Puppies
Puppy Book For Kids

Other Titles by Gary Dickinson

Books, Picture Books, Series Books

Birds of Prey: Owls!
A Bird Book About Owls Featuring The Barn, Snowy, Screech Owls and More,
With Amazing Pictures, Information And Fun Facts

Birds of Prey: Eagles!
A Bird Book About Eagles Featuring The Bald And Golden Eagles and More,
With Amazing Pictures And Information On Their Food, Habitat And Threats.

Birds: Children's Book With Amazing Pictures And Fun Facts About Booby Birds

Lighthouses For Kids
Tallest, Oldest, Spookiest And Famous Lighthouses! A Kids Book Of Fun And
Interesting Facts And Amazing Pictures Of Lighthouses

Flying! Airplanes, Aircraft & Space Travel
Flight From The Past, Present And To The Future With Fun Interesting Facts
And Over 100 Amazing Pictures All About Flight

Animals! Animal Books For Kids:
A Book Of Animal Facts And Animal Pictures About The Mammals,
Reptiles And Amphibians Of The Animal Kingdom

The Human Body: A Kids Book About Body Systems!
Learn Fun And Interesting Facts About Noises Our Body Makes And More

Storms, Extreme Weather

Thanksgiving, A Special Celebration

Christmas Traditions Around The World

Twelve Days of Christmas

Valentine's Day: I Love You

The Easter Story

Childrens' Picture Books

The Curious Ducklings
Kids Book Age 3: Opposites!
A Picture Book Featuring Jungle Animals To Teach Kids About Opposites

Maddix The Spunky Monkey Series

Maddix The Spunky Monkey Springs A Zoo Surprise

Maddix The Spunky Monkey's Halloween Surprise

Maddix The Spunky Monkey's Thanksgiving Turkey Trouble

Maddix The Spunky Monkey's Magical Christmas Book

Maddix The Spunky Monkey's Valentine's Day Surprise

Maddix The Spunky Monkey and the Easter Egg Surprise

Find them all here:

Puppies
Puppy Book For Kids

Learning The Fun Way To Love & Care For Your First Dog

GARY DICKINSON

DEDICATION

This book is about our Toy Poodle named Coco.

We got Coco from our local pet shop and she's enjoyed living in a loving caring home ever since.

Coco receives all the usual pet benefits and privileges such as wholesome meals, washes at home and regular grooming at her groomer.
She receives her tick and flea treatments, deworming tablets and regular vaccinations/inoculations that she needs to have.
She goes for daily walks and runs on the beach which she absolutely loves and laps up.
She also has a few of her own unique privileges such as sitting on any available lap she can find and sleeping on our bed at night to name a couple.

Some dogs do not enjoy this attention, love and affection.
Some dogs are mistreated, neglected and even abused.

This book is dedicated to those carers such as the Society for the Prevention of Cruelty to Animals (SPCA or similar) who take in and care for these dogs that don't have the luxury of a loving and caring home. Those that have been subjected to all manner of neglect and cruelty but have had the good fortune to have been taken in by these wonderful carers.

Dogs are amazing companions so full of the "joys of spring" in everything they do. They show us unconditional love at it's best.
We can learn so much from them if we'd just take the time to watch and observe these pets we call "man's best friend".

Thank-you to those that care.

CONTENTS

ACKNOWLEDGMENTS

Thank-you to my wonderful wife who has provided an abundance of photographs and her own insights and ideas when putting this short book together.

Thanks also to our friends Mark and Linda Clarkson, who not only "baby sat" our very new and young puppy shortly after we got her but also for the beautiful photographs they took of Coco doing fun things in the kitchen and garden while with them.

Chapter 1

INTRODUCTION

Puppies are so cute, cuddly and down right irresistible and Coco was no exception! From the moment we laid eyes on her, there was just that something about Coco that yelled out "TAKE ME HOME; TAKE ME HOME!!".

In his book, the author shares the joy of owning and taking care of Coco his Toy Poodle. The photos in this book have been "chosen by Coco" and taken out of Coco's personal portfolio just as they are. No photo-shopping, enhancing or manipulating in any shape or form. They will bring Coco alive and show her as authentic, cute and down right adorable!

Have you ever wanted your very own dog? Maybe to get a cute little puppy? They are so cuddly aren't they! You just want to hold them in your hands and cuddle them. They are so much fun but you have to remember that they are also hard work because you have to look after them and care for them too.

Coco Introduced

This is a story about my little dog that is so cute and has been lots of fun. Take a look at this very cute little ball of fluff. She's a Toy Poodle.

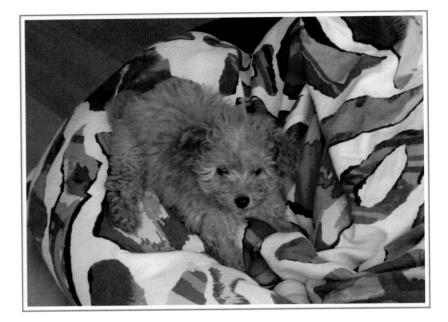

From the moment I saw her, I knew I wanted that little doggie with its cute looks and a little nose that looked just like a button.

Can you read what the shop wrote when I bought her?

I love my dog so much that I have decided to write a book about her for you, so that you can see how much fun it is to have a dog but also to learn how to care for your puppy. This story then, is about my very special little dog called Coco and our family.

I decided to call my little puppy Coco. That was because it reminded me of a yummy chocolate drink called cocoa.

Coco was so tiny when I got her. She could fit into the palm of our hands.

Do you know what a puppy's feet are called?

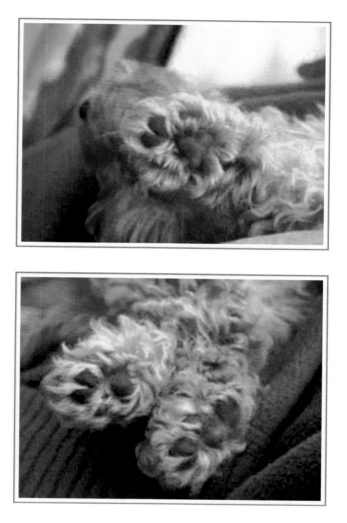

That's right. They're called paws. Look at Coco's cute little paws.

Here is Coco at the end of a long day at play…

She is able to sleep almost anywhere when she's so tired but she is most comfortable when she is sleeping on someone's lap. Especially if there is a nice warm blanket and fleecy top to keep her warm and comfortable.

Chapter 2

HAVING FUN

Coco was so much fun at home. She used to run and jump around all over the place and have lots of fun.

Look at these fun pictures of Coco when she was eight weeks old. In this first one, Coco looks like she's going to be part of the recipe sitting in the pot like that!

The slipper is way to big for Coco in this picture!

And here Coco is taking time to smell the flowers.

Looks like Coco is shouting "Hey! You missed a patch!"

Coco in the wheelbarrow

Look at Coco's ear how it is sticking up there. It looks like she's saying "what was that you said? Could you repeat that please!"

Puppies are just like little children. They love to have toys to play with and Coco' is no exception. Her favorite toy was a Teddy called Gregory.

Look how cute they are together. Don't you think they look alike!

When Coco was old enough, I could take her with me to the beach. This was her favorite place to play. It was like a HUGE sand pit for her to play in. In this picture you can see her digging at my foot. In this game, I would have to keep moving my foot for her to "dig out". She could play this game for hours and because she was still so small and I did not want her to run away, I kept her lead on her while she played.

Coco at play on the beach.

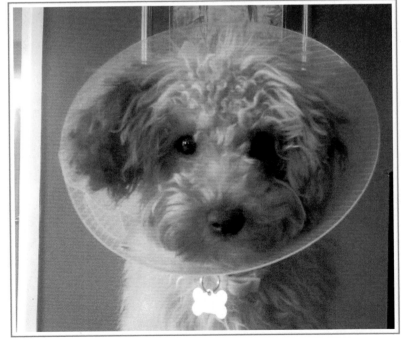

Doesn't Coco look funny wearing that cone!

When Coco was 6-months old, she had to have an operation. After the operation, I had to make sure that Coco did not lick her sore so the doctor said that she should wear that funny cone. While she had that cone on, she could not reach and lick her sore.

Chapter 3

SCHOOL, PLAY, SLEEP

When Coco was a puppy, I used to take her to puppy school so that she could learn to be a good, obedient dog. This was the beginning of her training.

It's very important that your dog is obedient else it won't listen to you when you ask it to do something for you. For example, it won't sit when you want your dog to sit or a very important command to obey is to come back to you when you call it. This is possibly one of the most, if not the most important command you will want you dog to obey.

It is also good for your dog to be able to get along with other dogs. For this reason, Coco used to go to a Doggie Day Care two times a week just so that she could learn how to be friendly with other dogs. You don't want a dog that is aggressive toward other dogs or animals.

Look at Coco in the next picture with her two friends on "their throne". It looks like they are all looking down at the big dogs below them. Coco seems to have taken up the prime position on the seat of the chair.

Here she is playing outside with other dogs.

In the picture below, can you see Coco playing in the sand pit with her friends? She's almost the same color as the sand.

As Coco got older and bigger I could take her to the beach without a lead and this is still her favorite place to go. The beach is like a HUGE sandpit for her to play in. She loves to play fetch with her ball but also still loves to dig big holes.

Here she is at play digging on the beach.

After a hard day playing on the beach, Coco would come

home and sleep. She would fall asleep anywhere but her favorite place is on her big soft and cuddly doggie toy, Snoopy.

See how Coco somehow managed to end up under Snoopy's arm. She did this all on her own. I was lucky to get this picture.

Did you know that puppies can sleep up to 20 hours a day? This depends on what kind of dog they are but they do sleep a lot as puppies.

Sometimes puppies get up to mischief when they get bored and do naughty things. When Coco was naughty I used to put her in the naughty corner.

Look at her sitting under the chair outside. She knew she had been naughty and sat there obediently until I called her inside.

You have to remember to play with your puppy often so they don't get into trouble just like Scampy and Lassie in these next pictures. Scampy likes cushions and Lassie likes pot plants. This is what happens when your puppy gets bored.

We are often tempted to be cross with our dogs when they do things like this but they are only being dogs and looking for something to do. They have loads of energy when they are young so it's important that you can keep them busy like playing games with them or taking them for a walk.

Even when they're naughty, they still look cute don't they! Look how Scampy is lying on top of all the insides of the pillow she has just pulled apart.

I don't think that Scampy nor Lassie will be able to blame the damage on anyone else. They have definitely been caught "red handed" haven't they!

Scampy. What have you done?

Lassie. Did you break that pot?

Chapter 4

TAKING CARE OF YOUR DOG

Owning a dog also means you have to take good care of your pet and sometimes your puppy can get sick or, like this poor dog here, it can hurt itself. Look how its friend is playing nurse.

One time Coco's eye got sore because sand got into her eye from digging and playing on the beach. Can you see how her right eye is closing?

I couldn't see what was wrong so I had to take her to the animal doctor.

Do you know what an animal doctor is called? Yes, that's right. An animal doctor is called a veterinarian but that's such a long word, I call him a vet instead, like the one here. Do you have another name for your pet's doctor?

Image courtesy Dr. Max FB Page

The vet put some drops in her eyes that made them go a funny color so that he could see if anything was wrong with them or if something was maybe stuck in her eye.

What color did her eyes go? Can you see? Look carefully at the picture on the next page for the answer.

Yes they went a green color so she looked a bit like a martian.

Coco loves her balls. I am always kicking or throwing a ball for her to chase after. In fact, when she wants to play with her ball, she will often bring it to me and drop it on my lap or sometimes next to me. Then she hops off the chair and just stands looking very intently at me, willing us to pick up the ball and throw it for her.

Look at Coco sitting on her chair with all her balls. How many balls can you see?

Do you remember me saying that you need to keep your dog busy? Playing with the balls is a very good way to exercise your pet and in my case, to exercise Coco.

Just like Coco, most dogs love balls so you can do the same by taking your dog to a park or beach and throwing the ball for it to fetch. Coco loves playing fetch.

Look at Doris in the next picture. As you can see, Coco isn't the only one that loves playing with balls.

How many balls has Doris fetched in her mouth… all at once?

Chapter 5

WASHING AND GROOMING

It is also important to wash your dog. If your dog is scratching itself, one reason could be that it may need a bath. Of course another reason could be just because it's dirty from playing in the mud like these dogs here.

You can wash your dog in lots of different places. Look at these different baths.

This one fits in a bucket.

Look at these twins with their shower caps on in the bath. If you had 2 twin dogs like these, what would you call them?

Can you see how many ducks are outside Jessie's tub?

Doesn't Scotty look like he's enjoying his bath. Scotty is being washed in the sink.

Coco goes to a groomer every six weeks to get her hair cut as well as her nails. Yes, dogs also need to cut their nails.

When Coco comes back from having a wash and shampoo and her hair cut, she always comes back looking pretty. Take a look at these different looks.

Look at the first picture to see what Coco looked like before she had her first hair cut.

And this is what she looked like after her groom! Which picture do you prefer?

Sometimes it gets very cold for Coco because she's so small. Especially in winter. So I put a lovely warm jumper or coat on her like these ones here.

Can you read what is on her jumper in this picture?

That's right. It says "Sweet Stuff" and it's so true. She is very sweet indeed.

You can also have fun dressing your dog up.

What is the pink jacket called here that Coco is wearing here so she does not get wet when it rains?

Look at this funny doggie Daisy the way she is dressed . She even has some funny little shoes on.

When you're away

It is very important to find someone who will look after your dog and love your dog just as much as you do when you go away on holidays.

When I go away on holiday, Coco goes to her favorite granny who spoils her so much. Here Coco is all packed and ready to go on her holiday, and she always takes her best toy with her. Do you remember the name of her favorite toy dog? This is the one in the photo with her here?

When she goes to her granny, they often sit and watch television together and eat snacks.

Coco and granny having a chat… or maybe Coco is just looking to see what there is for her to eat!

Granny and Coco watching television.

Chapter 6

TRANSPORT

If you take your dog in the car it is important to make sure they are strapped in safely just like you and like little Benjy in the photo.

There are many ways to strap your dog in safely. The one in the picture above is a seat strap that locks and fastens into the safety belt buckle.

Another way that some people keep their dogs safe is to buy a small "cage" that they put into the back of their car. This prevents them falling off the seat when driving and also prevents them being thrown forward if the car has to stop suddenly.

Other people have a safety net or screen fitted that separates the rear of the car (in a station wagon kind of car) from the passenger area. This is also an excellent way to keep the dogs safe in the back. It is particularly useful for larger dogs.

Remember though, no matter which way you secure your dogs, they can't open and close windows if they are hot. They also need water more frequently than we do so you need to make sure that they are comfortable when they are in the car. Open a window for them - they love wind blowing in their face. It's a way for them to enjoy the ride by smelling the air.

Chapter 7

TRAINING

Coco often has a friend Rosie that comes and visits. They eat and play together.

Just like we learn good manners, it is very important when your dogs eat that they sit and wait for their food until you tell them that they can eat.

You must also remember to always put water out for your dog so that they have something to drink when they get thirsty.

Dogs love treats too. You use treats when you want to teach them obedience or even new tricks. See how good Coco is lying down.

Coco, Down

Good Girl

Let's try a few more tricks like "sit", "high five", "pray" or even "dance"?

Coco, Sit

Coco, High Five

Coco, Pray

Coco, Dance

One of Cocos favorite games is to play hide and seek. Can you find Coco in these pictures?

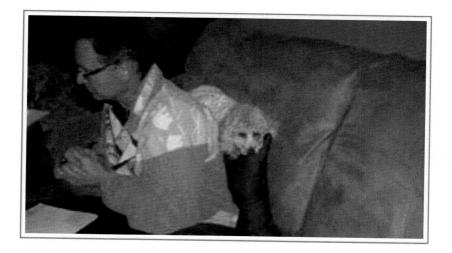

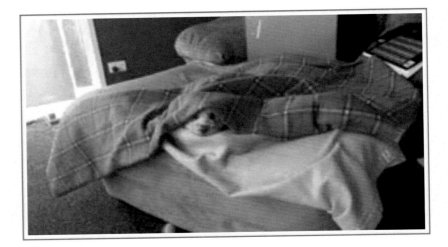

So remember that just as you like to play with your friends, your doggie also LOVES to play. Make time to play with your dog regularly.

One of Coco's favorite times of the year is Christmas as she loves dressing up and getting presents.

Who do you think she looks like? Can you see what presents she got for Christmas?

As you can see, having a dog is so much fun. You can play with them and they can give you lots of laughs.

But, just as much as you can play and have fun with them, you also have to love and care for your dog by feeding them, washing them, exercising them, taking them to the doctor if they are sick and even cleaning up after them. If you do all of that, you and your dog will be in for a long and loving relationship. They will be your best friend.

For me, Coco gives me lots of laughs and I love having her with me in my home. She definitely has become my best friend and part of the family. Here we are altogether at Christmas time.

Wishing you every bit of happiness, joy, companionship and friendship with your dog, that our little Coco has given to us.

The End

ABOUT THE AUTHOR

Gary Dickinson always felt there was at least one book 'inside him'. In 2013 he traded the corporate world for the life of a writer, and today shares his diverse interests through his children's books. His love of nature is captured in his series of books on birds, mammals, reptiles and amphibians, while his passion for planes has generated a series on aviation.

Gary's books are read and loved by children around the world, and Gary brings his stories to life to inspire a new generation of adventurers and nature lovers.

Gary's philosophy is simple: you don't need to go far for adventure - if you look closely, you'll find it right on your doorstep!